Acknowledgement

This book introduces children to the DRSABCD action plan in a simplified, age-appropriate way to help them recognise danger, respond to emergencies, and seek help with confidence. The steps are inspired by evidence-based first aid practices, such as those published by Australia Wide First Aid (2022).

Reference

Australia Wide First Aid. (2022). What is DRSABCD? | Definition & Action Plan. Retrieved from https://www.australiawidefirstaid.com.au/resources/what-is-drsabcd

Copyright:

© 2025 Kasey Lee

All rights reserved. No part of this publication may be reproduced, distributed, or transmitted in any form or by any means, including photocopying, recording, or other electronic or mechanical methods, without the prior written permission of the publisher, except in the case of brief quotations embodied in critical reviews and certain other non-commercial uses permitted by copyright law.

For permission requests, contact:

Kasey Lee at Nurtured Brave.
NurturedBrave@gmail.com

For my babies- Aylah and Kooper,
and my nieces and nephews.
You are my greatest inspiration and the bravest little heroes I know.
Your curiosity, courage, and big hearts inspire me every day.
This book is for you —
a reminder that you have the power to be calm, brave, and kind in everything you do.
With all my love.

IS FOR DANGER

Look around with your superhero eyes,
Are there any dangers? Any surprise?
If it's not safe, we don't go near.
We stay back and call for help from here.

IS FOR RESPONSE

Say hello and give a tap,
"Are you okay?" Just like that.
Then ask these questions, nice and slow:
"Can you hear me?"
"Open your eyes."
"What's your name?"
If they don't talk or move at all,
It's time to send for help, make that call!

IS FOR
SEND FOR HELP

No time to wait, it's time to go,
Find a grown up or call ooo!
Say what you see and where you are,
Try to stay calm like a mighty star.

IS FOR
AIRWAY

Check their airway, nice and wide,
No blocks or bumps should be inside.
Stay close, stay calm, don't touch or steer,
A grown-up helper will soon be here.

IS FOR
BREATHING

Watch their chest and listen near,
Can you feel, see or hear?
If they're not breathing, don't delay.
We're brave and ready to help today.

IS FOR

CPR

Place two fingers gently on
their wrist to feel for a beat,
If there's no thump, your help is what they need!
Push hard and fast in the middle of the chest,
Keep pumping strong, that works the best!
Don't stop or fear, just keep the pace,
Help is coming to take your place.

IS FOR
DEFIBRILLATOR

If someone brings a special box,
With sticky pads and flashing shocks,
Let the grown-ups take the lead,
You've done your best in someone's time of need.

YOU DID IT!

YOU WERE MIGHTY BRAVE.

You stayed calm, you did your part,
Helping others with all your heart.
Being brave is what you do,
The world is safer, thanks to YOU!

You might feel PROUD, or TIRED too,
with big brave feelings shining through.
It's okay, feelings come along,
BRAVE people feel them all day long.
Find your safe person, tell them it all,
the big, the brave, the proud, the small.
They'll listen close and help you through,
that's what MIGHTY HEARTS all do.
Now take a breath, your brave is true,
I'm sharing a HUG from me to you.

BREATHING

AIRWAY

BE MIGHTY

BE BRAVE

RESPONSE

CERTIFICATE OF BRAVERY

THIS CERTIFIES THAT YOU ARE MIGHTY BRAVE!

THIS CERTIFICATE IS PROUDLY PRESENTED TO

_____

For showing mighty courage and a brave heart when learning DRSABCD. Your bravery inspires others and shows that even the smallest heroes can do big, mighty things!

Awarded on: _____
Presented by: *Kasey Lee*
Founder of Nurtured Brave.

BE MIGHTY BE BRAVE

Kasey Lee is a Registered Nurse and proud mother to two little superheroes,
who inspired her to create Be Mighty, Be Brave.
Her children are the heart behind her work, sparking the creation of Nurtured Brave
—a space dedicated to empowering kids with safety, confidence, and courage.
With a passion for teaching children that they are capable of amazing things,
Kasey wrote this story to gently introduce first response skills through rhyme and play.
She hopes every child who reads it will discover that even the smallest superheroes
can make a mighty difference.

www.ingramcontent.com/pod-product-compliance
Lightning Source LLC
Chambersburg PA
CBHW041201290426
44109CB00002B/90